KinderSounds: Rebus Readers

by Lillian Lieberman

illustrated by Marilynn Barr

Publisher: Roberta Suid
Copy Editor: Carol Whiteley
Design and Production: Little Acorn Associates, Inc.
Cover Design: David Hale

Entire contents copyright © 2001 by Monday Morning Books, Inc.,
Box 1680, Palo Alto, California 94302
For a complete catalog, write to the address above.

Call our toll-free number: 1-800-255-6049
E-mail us at: MMBooks@aol.com
Visit our Web site:
http://www.mondaymorningbooks.com

monday morning ®

ISBN 1-57612-128-3

Printed in the United States of America
9 8 7 6 5 4 3 2 1

Contents

Introduction

KinderSounds: Rebus Readers presents 22 emergent mini-readers for children aged preschool to kindergarten. The readers use high-frequency words accompanied by rebus pictures. The words and simple phrases are repeated to make the readers predictable, and the rebus pictures add high interest to the content. The simple format makes these books ideal for use by teachers and parents who are initiating children into the world of reading.

The mini-readers in *KinderSounds: Rebus Readers* start out with words, then progress to short phrases, and gradually build to simple sentences. The different types of rebus sentences mimic real language patterns by asking a question, giving a command, or exclaiming—all part of the first reading experience.

The teacher guides the children through the readers. Each story is first read to the children, with the children following. The children echo the words and name the pictures that show familiar objects, animals, people, actions, or activities. The repetition of words helps children to predict and soon read the high-frequency words. The pictures carry out the whimsical content and invite the children to become active participants in the reading process. Children will want to read each reader several times for enjoyment as well as reinforcement. A handy glossary at the end of each reader lists the words used and names the rebus pictures. Suggestions and steps for using the readers are given in the "How to Use Rebus Readers" section.

Many of the readers focus on a theme that children can identify with, such as "A Party," "The Beach," and "A Circus." Others play on the words presented in the story. For example, in the reader "Go!" a familiar race is run between a rabbit and a turtle. Of course, the turtle wins! Children will delight in some of the subtle endings to the readers. For instance, in "Stop," the Gingerbread Boy actually gets away in a boat. In "My Hat," the last hat turns out to be a nest full of baby chicks. And in "The Bug," the bug ends up on the child's nose! The humor woven into the stories will tickle the children's imaginations.

Rebus Readers can be used flexibly to suit the developmental level of the young child in the mainstream classroom as well as in the special resource classroom.

How to Make Rebus Readers

Duplicate the pages for each Rebus Reader. Cut the pages apart and place the pages in the correct number order. Trim if necessary. For the cover, cut construction paper or colored copy paper in half. Insert the Rebus Reader pages. Staple along the left side of the cover. Write the title of the reader on the front cover with felt pen or colored crayons or pencils. Be sure to place a protective sheet under the cover page when writing with felt pen.

Make a set of Rebus Readers for each child or keep a set in the classroom for children to use. Children may store their own sets in shoe boxes to read independently after guided reading. They may enjoy reading with a partner in their free time. Rebus Readers are ideal for children to take home to share with family and friends.

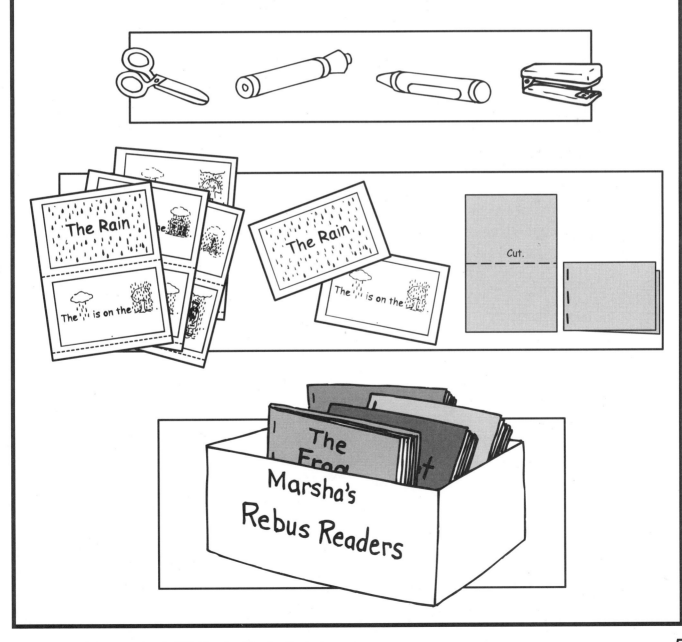

How to Use Rebus Readers

Reading Preparation

Before reading a Rebus Reader, have the children look at the title page and the pictures and briefly talk about what the reader may be about. The glossary at the end of the reader may be used to study the reader's words and name the rebus pictures.

Guiding the Reading

When you read the story, encourage the children to echo the words and supply the names for the rebus pictures. On the second and later readings, start by reading the first page, then see if the children can read the next pages independently. The repeated words make this an easy task. Provide the words when assistance is needed. Encourage the children to read with expression to add meaning to the text.

During each reading, talk about the story contents. Ask specific guiding questions to help children read with understanding, read "between the lines," and interpret picture clues. Ask who, what, when, where, why, and how questions to guide children to "read" with meaning.

After each reading, encourage the children to go over the glossary words and the rebus pictures. Words that are volunteered are also acceptable. Invite the children to read the readers many times over to acquire some sight word knowledge as well as some initial sound orientation. Initial phonemic awareness can be included by capitalizing on some of the sound elements. For instance, children can name as many words as they can that begin like the word *hug* when you read the "Hugs" reader. Or they can think of words that begin with the beginning blend in *frog* for "The Frog." They can even clap out and count the syllables for rebus picture names.

The themes of the readers can be extended and connected with the children's own experiences. For instance, children can share what they themselves can do after reading "I Can!" They can discuss additional things they associate with rain for "The Rain" and share something about their own pets when they read "My Pet."

Using the readers flexibly and creatively will make this initial reading experience enjoyable and meaningful.

Words for Rebus Readers

a	am	and	big	can
go	hug	I	in	is
like	my	no	not	on
pet	put	said	stop	ten
the	to	yes	yum	

Numbers

2 3 4 5

KinderSounds: Rebus Readers © 2001 Monday Morning Books, Inc.

A Party

a

2

a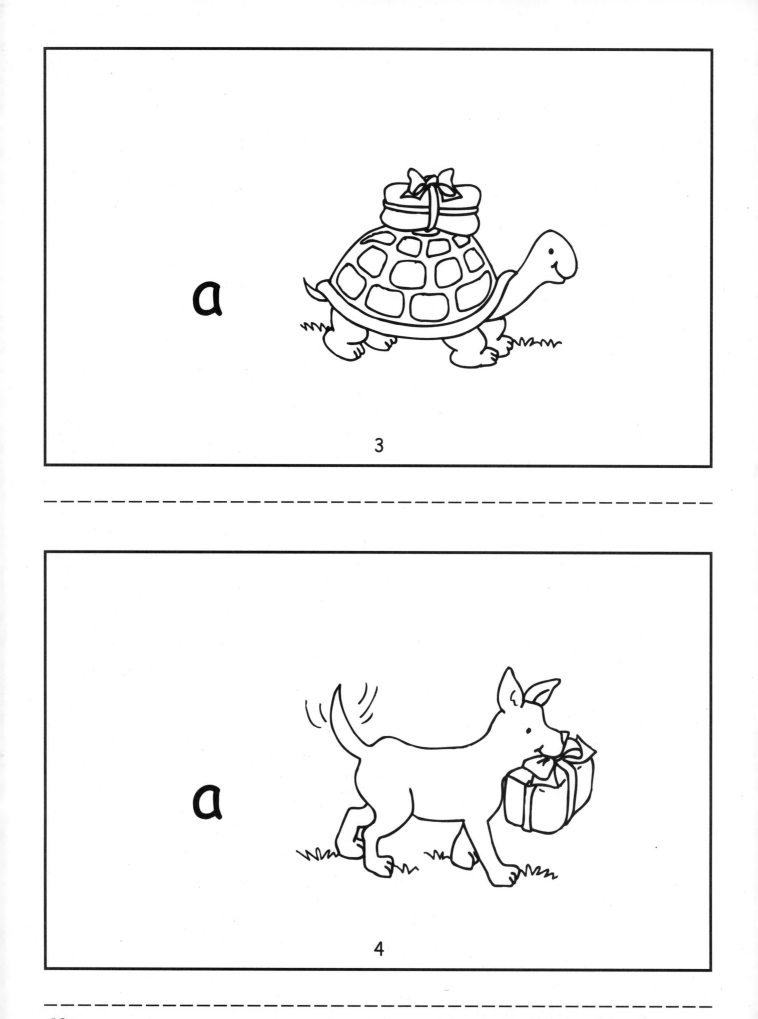

3

a

4

a

5

a

6

a

7

A Party
a

rabbit

turtle

dog

duck

bird

party

8

Beehive

a

2

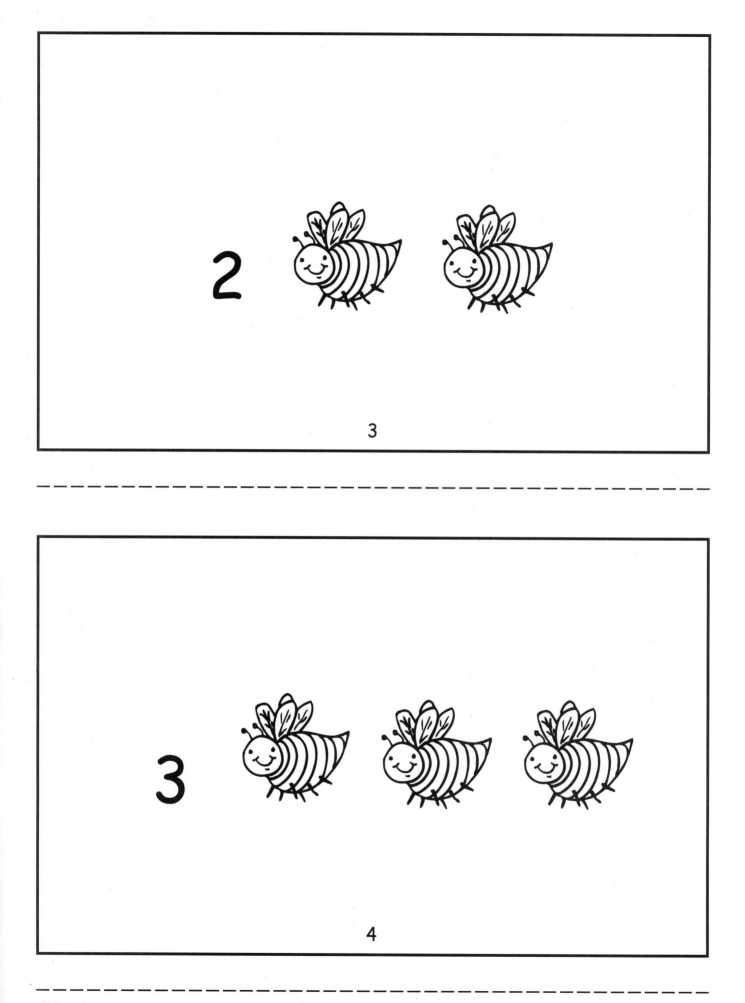

2

3

3

4

KinderSounds: Rebus Readers © 2001 Monday Morning Books, Inc.

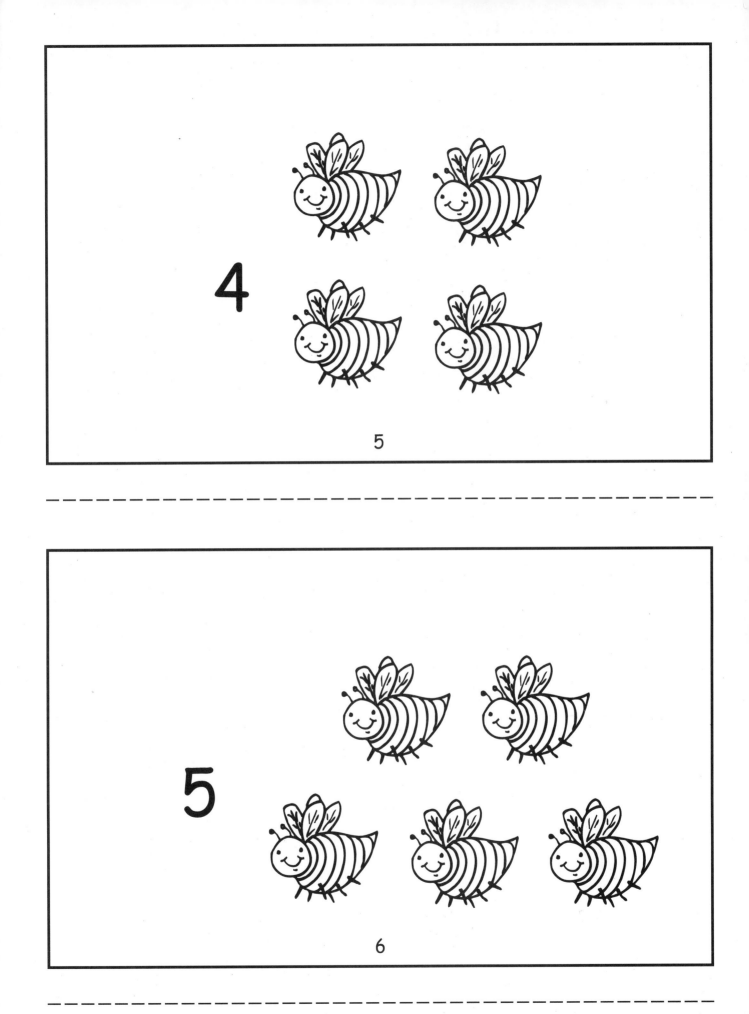

4

5

5

6

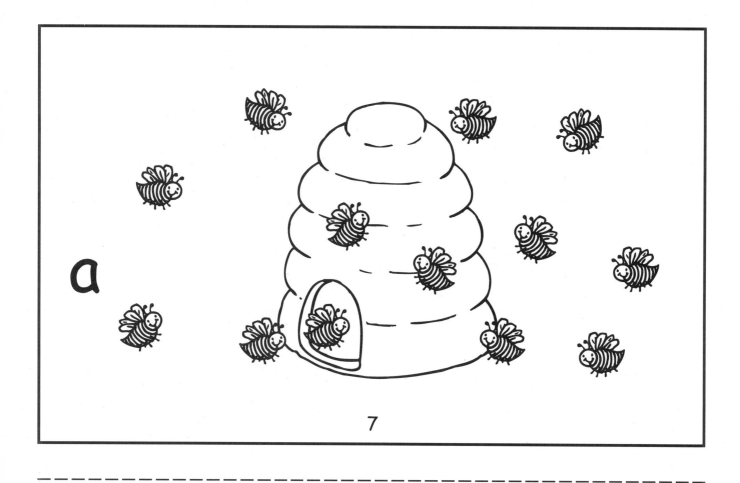

a

7

Beehive

a 2 3 4 5

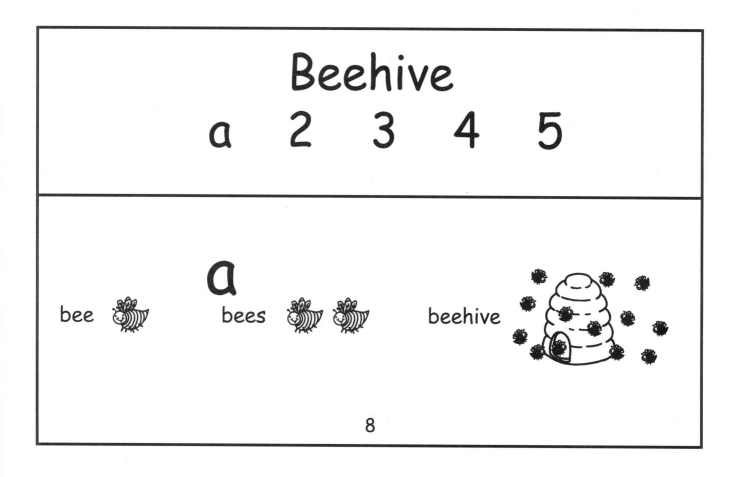

bee bees beehive

a

8

The Beach

the

2

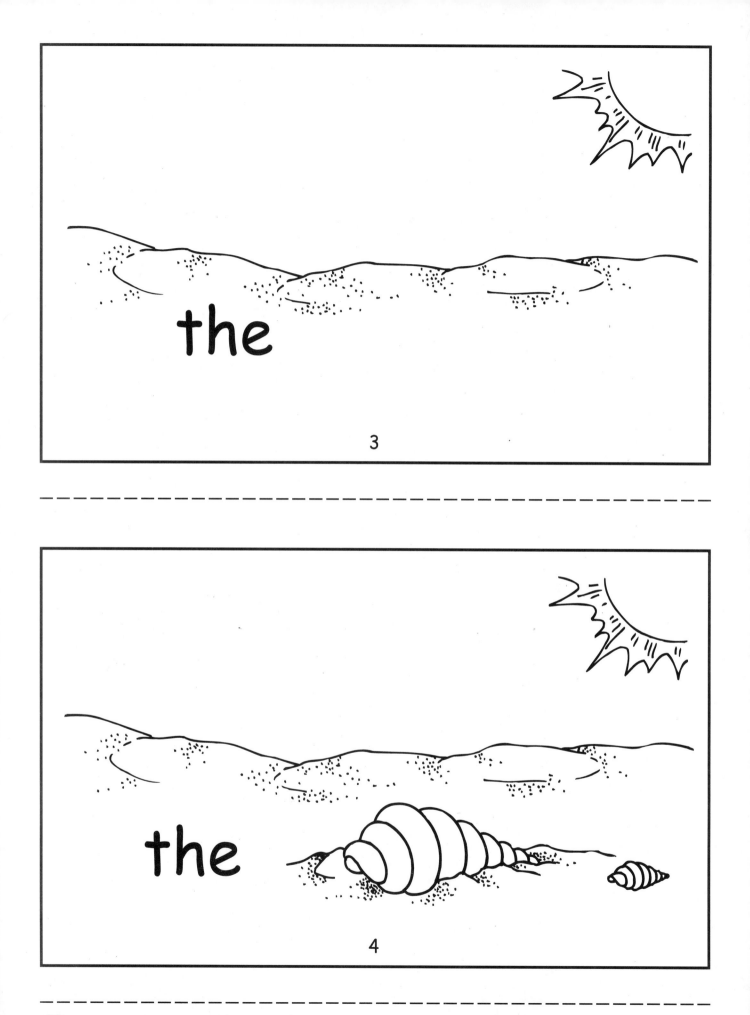

the

3

the

4

the

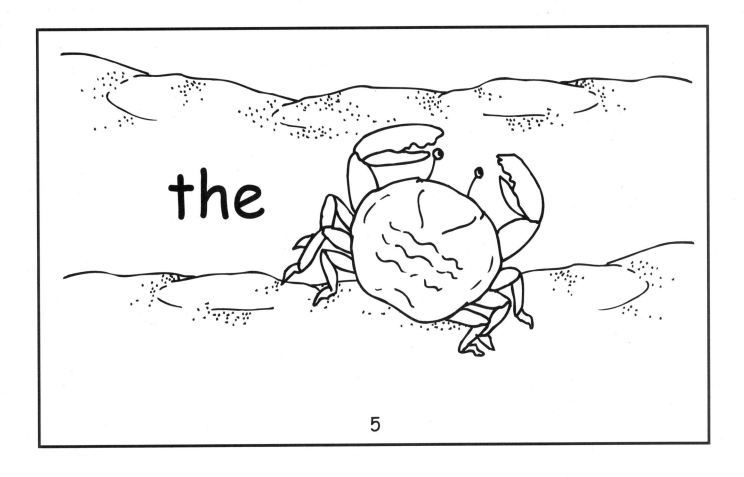

5

---

the

6

the

7

The Beach
the

ocean	sand	shell
crab	umbrella	beach

8

KinderSounds: Rebus Readers © 2001 Monday Morning Books, Inc.

My Hat

my

2

my

3

my

4

my

5

my

6

my

7

My Hat
my

hat   hat   hat

hat   hat   hat

8

KinderSounds: Rebus Readers © 2001 Monday Morning Books, Inc.

Go!

Go, go!

2

Go,   go!

3

Go,   go!

4

 KinderSounds: Rebus Readers © 2001 Monday Morning Books, Inc.

Go, go!

5

Go, go!

6

Go, go!

7

Go!
go

turtle   rabbit

8

To School

to

2

to

3

to

4

to

5

to

6

to

7

To School
to

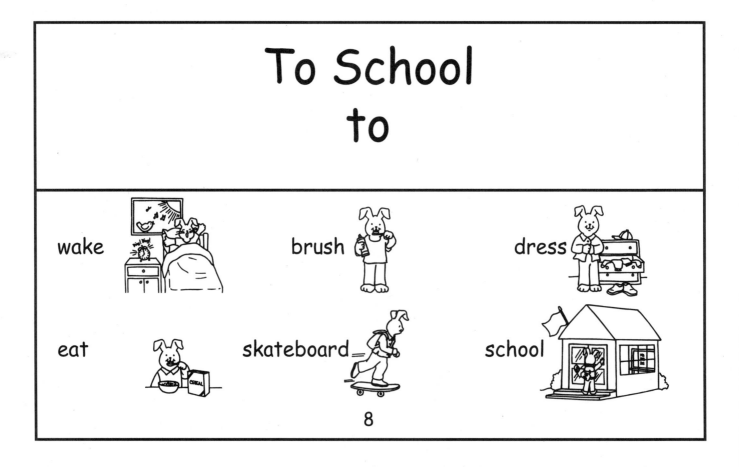

wake

brush

dress

eat

skateboard

school

8

Ten

ten

2

ten

3

ten

4

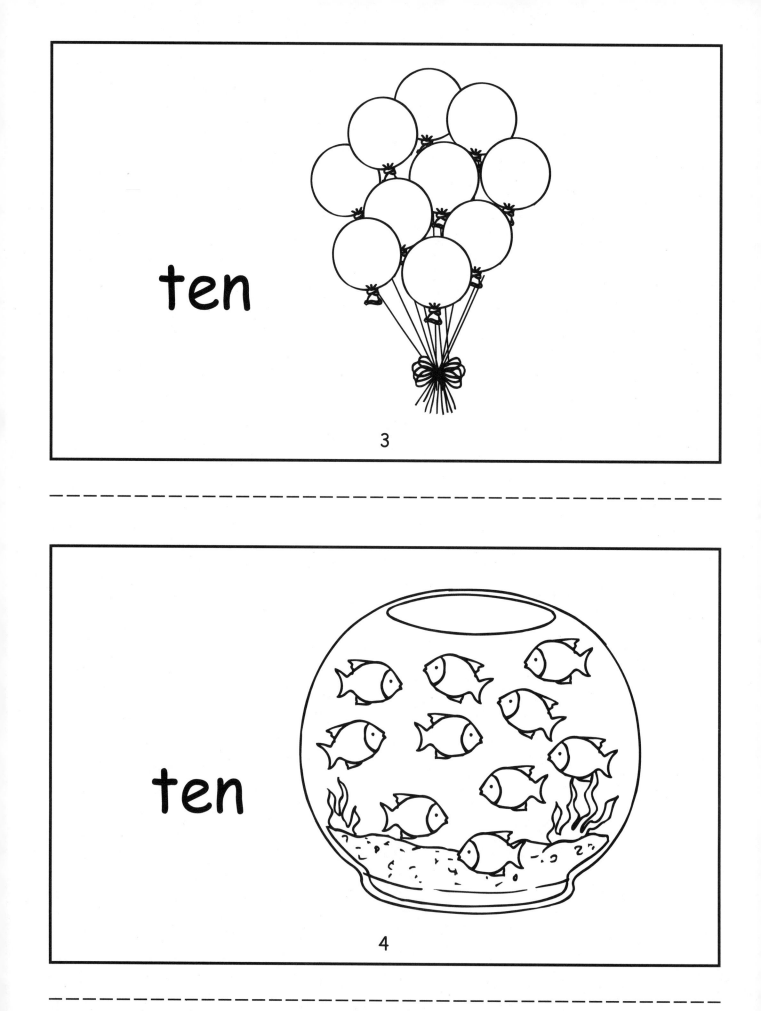

ten

5

ten

6

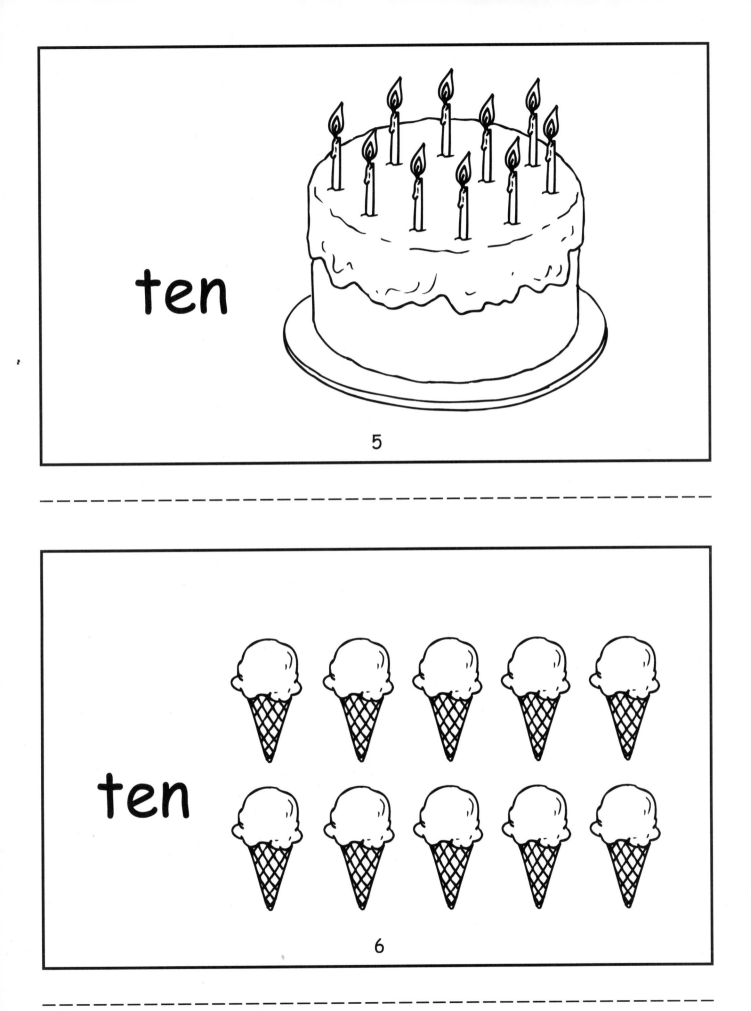

ten

7

Ten

ten

stars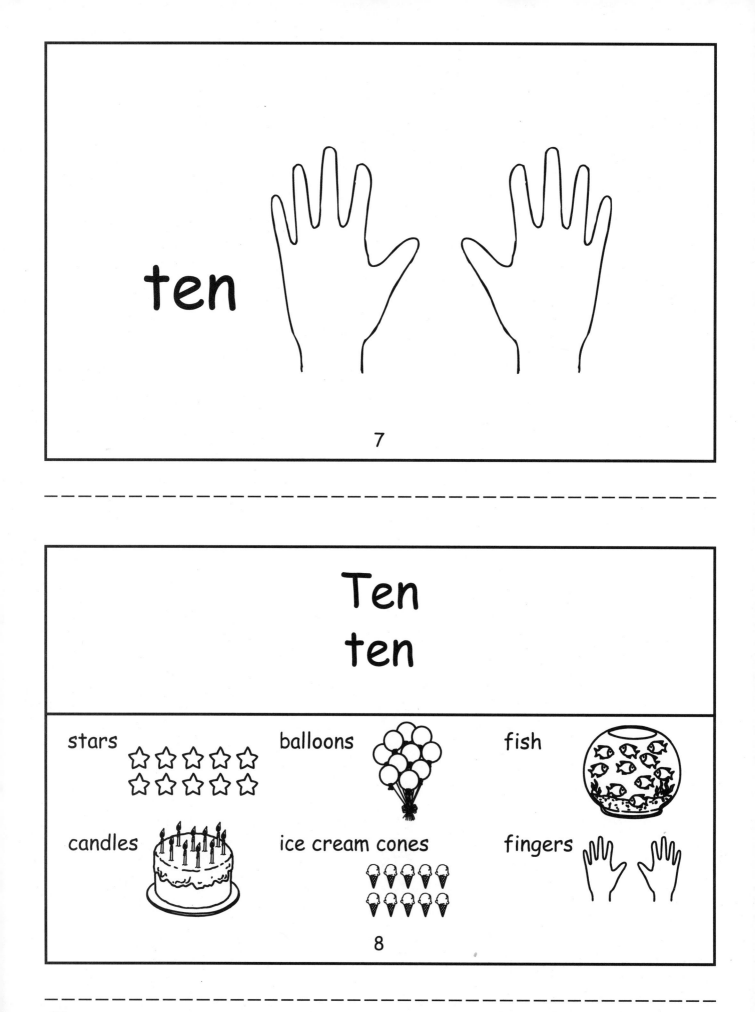

balloons

fish

candles

ice cream cones

fingers

8

The Bug

on the

2

on the

3

on the

4

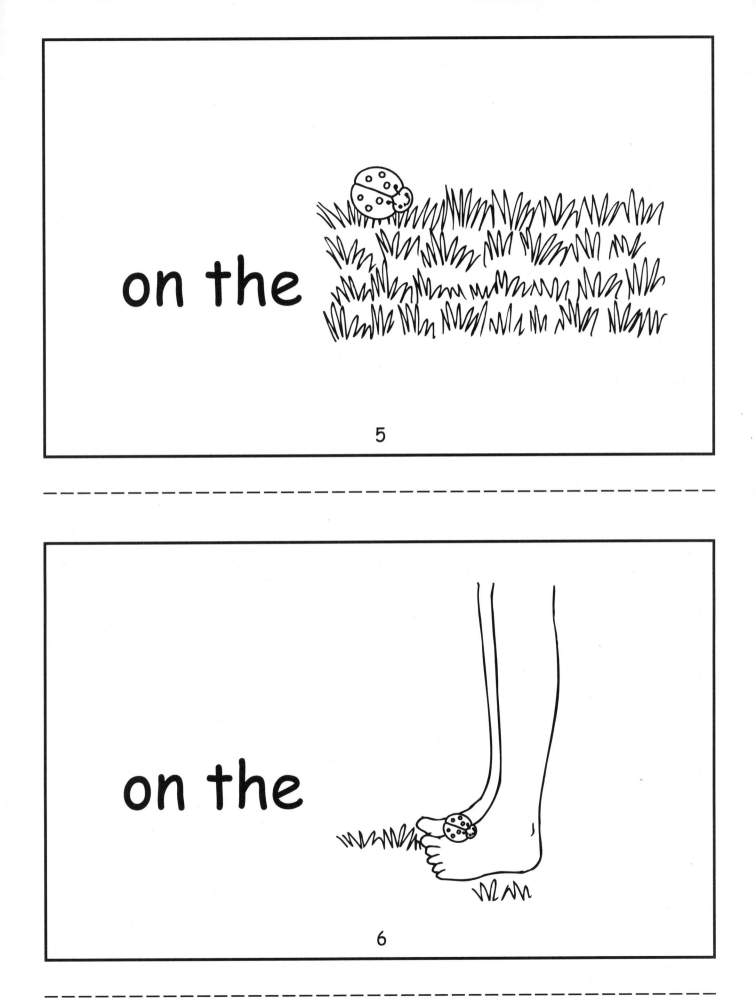

on the

5

- -

on the

6

- -

on the

7

The Bug
on the

leaf    flower    rock

grass    feet    nose

8

A Circus

a 🔴 and a 🦭

2

a  and a

3

a and a

4

a  and a

5

a and a

6

a

7

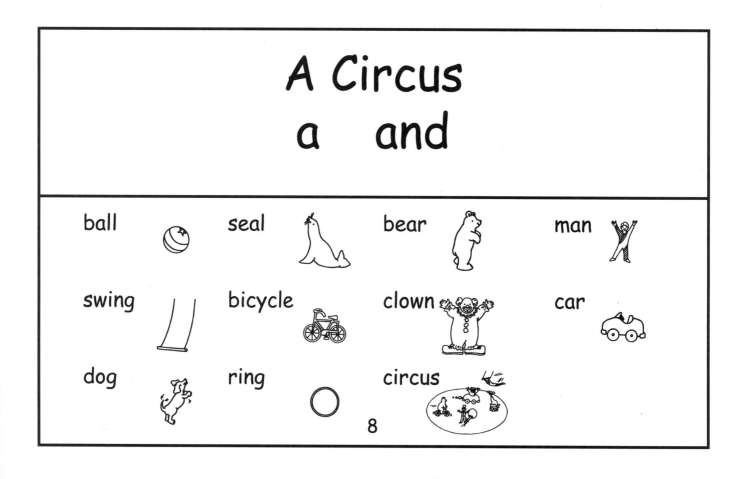

A Circus
a   and

ball 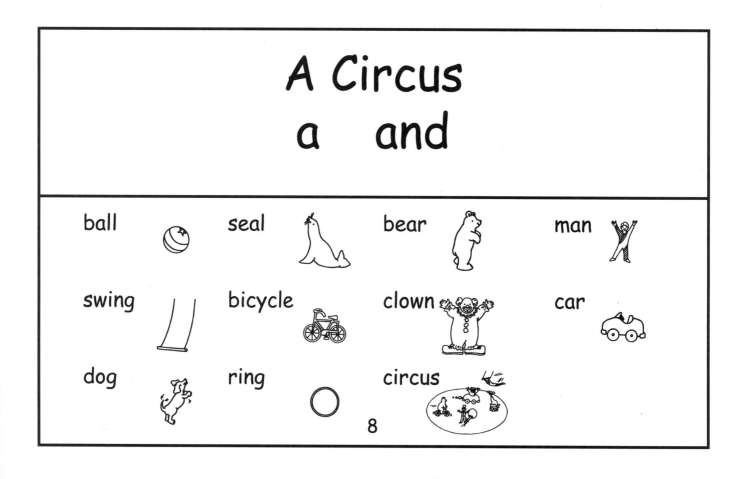   seal   bear   man

swing   bicycle   clown   car

dog   ring   circus

8

I Am!

I am a ⬚ .

2

I am a  .

3

I am a .

4

I am a  .

5

I am a .

6

I am a  .

7

I Am

a   am   I

cat   robot   rabbit

football player   dancer   monster

8

I Can!

I can  .

2

I can  .

3

I can .

4

I can  .

5

I can ____ .

6

I can 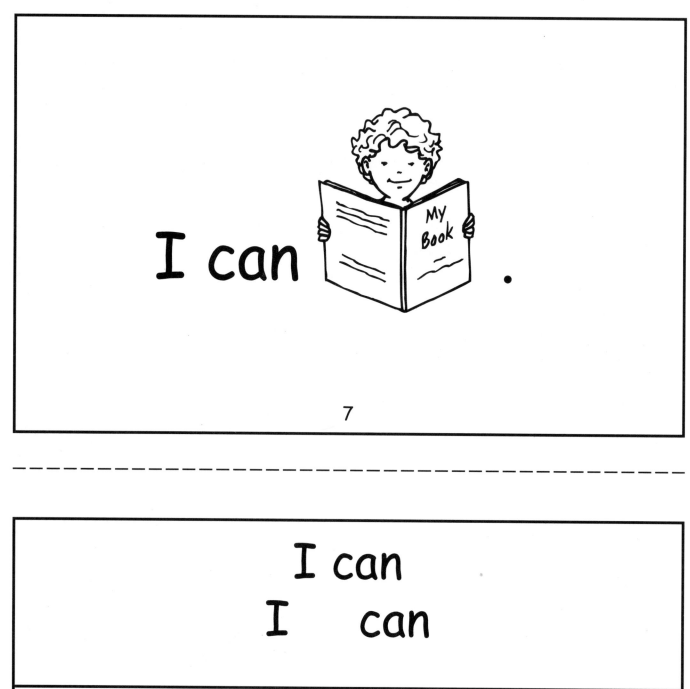 .

7

I can
I   can

jump 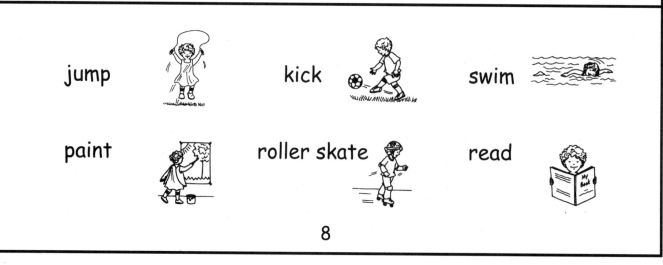 kick swim

paint roller skate read

8

I Like

I like   .

2

I like  .

3

I like .

4

I like  .

5

I like .

6

I like ____ .

7

I like

I   like

rainbows   ice cream   popcorn

dogs   butterflies   hugs

8

KinderSounds: Rebus Readers © 2001 Monday Morning Books, Inc.

👀→

I See!

I 👀 a 🌳 .

2

I 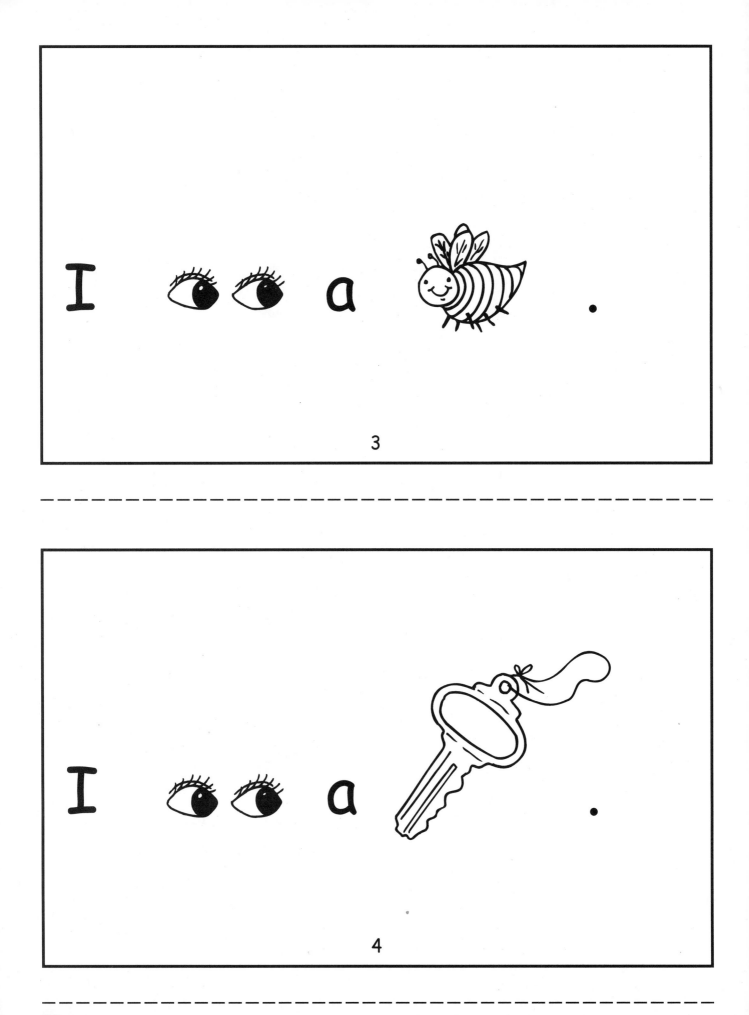 a 🐝 .

3

- -

I 👀 a 🔑 .

4

I 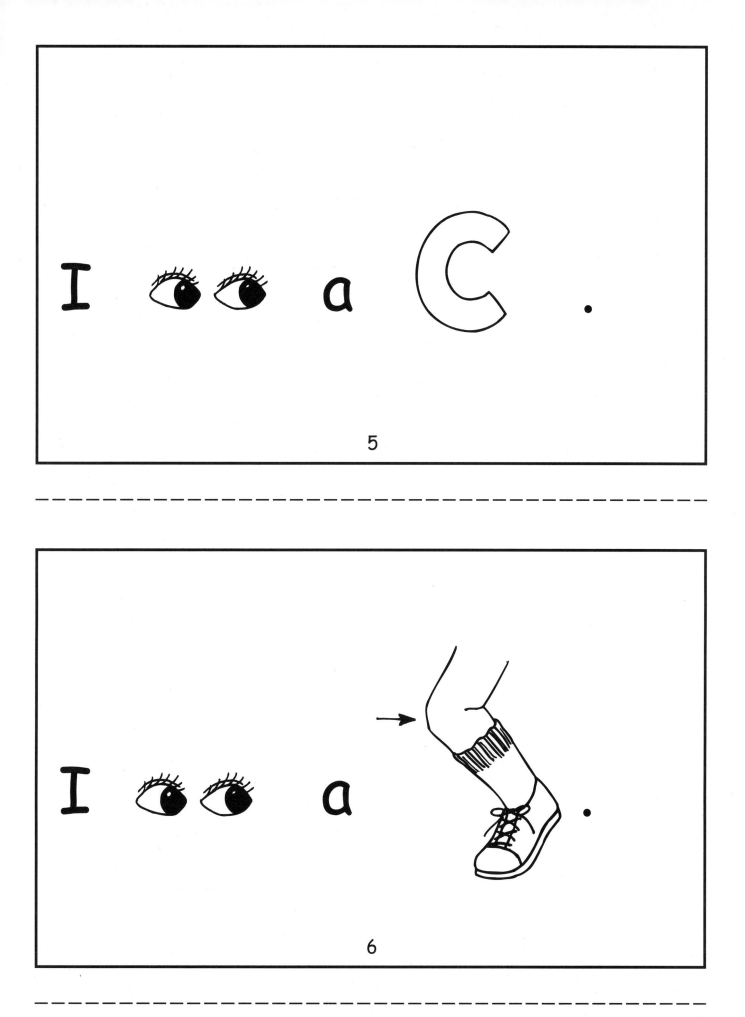 a C .

5

I 👁👁 a .

6

I 👁👁 .

7

I See!
a   I

see 👁👁   tree 🌳   bee 🐝

key 🔑   c   knee   me

8

Big

My is big.

2

My  is big.

3

My is big.

4

My  is big.

5

My is big.

6

My  is big.

7

Big
big   is   my

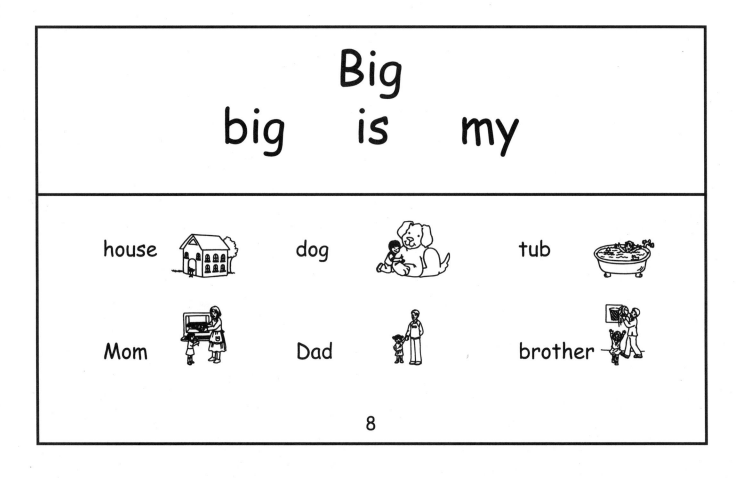

house   dog   tub

Mom   Dad   brother

8

The Frog

The  can  .

2

The  can .

3

The can .

4

The  can .

5

The can .

6

The [frog] can [hide] .

7

The Frog
the can

frog

jump

swim

catch

sleep

dive

hide

8

Up and Down

I can go   .

2

I can go  .

3

I can go .

4

I can go  .

5

I can go .

6

I can go .

7

Up and Down
can   go   I

up

up

up

down

down

down

8

Hugs

I can hug my  .

2

I can hug my  .

3

I can hug my .

4

I can hug my  .

5

I can hug my .

6

I can not hug a .

7

Hugs

a   can   hug   I   my   not

teddy bear   dog   cat

Mom   baby sister   skunk

8

The Rain

The [cloud with rain] is on the [tree in rain] .

2

The ☁ is on the 🏠 .

3

The ☁ is on the 🐌 .

4

The  is on the .

5

The is on the .

6

The __ is on the __ .

7

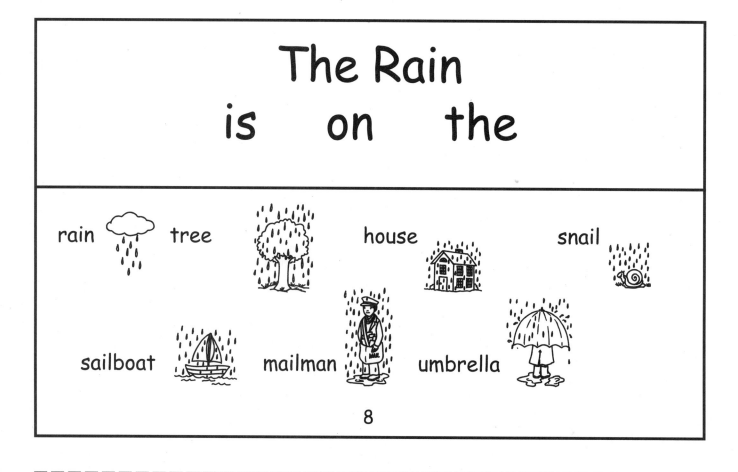

The Rain
is   on   the

rain   tree   house   snail

sailboat   mailman   umbrella

8

The Mouse

The 🐭 is in the 🐭.

2

The  is in the .

3

The is in the .

4

The  is in the .

5

The is in the .

6

The  is in the .

7

The Mouse
in   is   the

mouse   hole   box   dish

cheese   book   bed

8

KinderSounds: Rebus Readers © 2001 Monday Morning Books, Inc.

My Pet

Is the  my pet? No!

2

Is the  my pet? No!

3

Is the my pet? No!

4

Is the  my pet? No!

5

Is the my pet? No!

6

Is the 🐭 my pet? Yes!

7

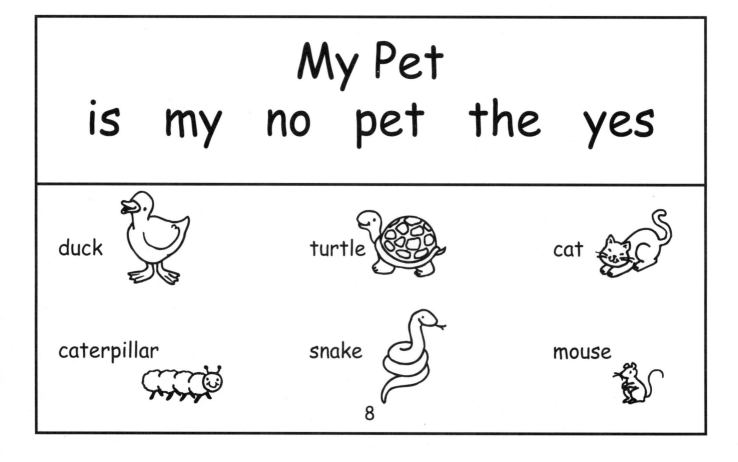

My Pet

is   my   no   pet   the   yes

duck

turtle

cat

caterpillar

snake

mouse

8

A Sandwich

Put on the  .

2

Put on the  .

3

Put on the .

4

Put on the  .

5

Put on the .

6

A  ! Yum!

7

A Sandwich

a   on   put   the   yum

butter

meat

cheese

tomatoes

lettuce

sandwich

8

Stop

"Stop," said the

2

"Stop," said the ⬡  .

3

"Stop," said the ⬡ .

4

"Stop," said the  .

5

"Stop," said the .

6

"Stop," said the   .

Stop

said   stop   the

lady   boy   dog

man   bird   fox   Stop